C
EXPLANATION
of
SALVATION

TIMOTHY R. CARTER

ISBN-13: 978-1977538826 ISBN-10: 1977538827

Scripture references taken from:

New Revised Standard Version (NRSV) is used for the study section.

King James Version (KJV) is used for the sermon.

The Message is used in the last section.

The New Living Translation (NLT) is used in the last section.

The Greek New Testament used *The Greek New Testament with Greek-English Dictionary (Ancient Greek Edition).* Hendrickson Publishers (2006). It is used to show the Greek origin for word study.

Cover Design: Rebecovers

[www.fiverr.com/rebecacovers]

This sermon has been printed to use as the author's own sermon notes. The purchaser may use these sermon notes as a study guide to preach in your own local pulpit where you are serving.

I dedicate this book to my homiletics professor, John A. Lombard, Jr. Thank you for the years of commitment that you poured into me. I can never thank you enough for the things that you taught me. I know that when you get to heaven you will receive something special for your investment.

Printed in the United States of America

Acknowledgments

This book comes as a result of Christian leaders pouring into me throughout my life.

Thank you to my dear friend Dr. Jeremy Love for your kindness in proofreading and advice through the years.

Thank you to my friend Stacy Schaller for your proofreading and help with this book.

Thank you, Marie O'Toole for your professionalism with editing this manuscript.

A special thanks goes to my parents Bishop Roy and Revonda Carter for raising me in the love of Christ.

Disclaimer

I have used the masculine pronoun in reference to both the believer and the sinner for easy reading. This is in no way meant to exclude females.

Table of Contents

Chapter One: Getting Started

THIS BOOK PRESENTS you with my research as I prepared a sermon from Romans 6:1-7. This exegetical study of the passage will give you the benefit of walking with me as I dig into the Word. This book also points you to the resource material used to learn from this passage.

In this section I draw out the meaning of Romans 6:1-7 and unfold it in a way that I hope will inspire and encourage you. In the following section, I have included the full manuscript of the sermon prepared from said study. Following the sermon, you will find a discussion on being saved by grace. Next, you will find a short comparison of what it means to be saved versus what it means to be a sinner. In the last section, you will learn how to meet Christ as your personal Savior.

Outline of the Exegetical Process

I. Introduction

    A. Why study this passage?

    B. Thesis statement

II. Historical Context in General

    A. Author, audience, date, occasion

    B. Sociological-cultural-religious background

III. Literary Context in General

    A. Genre of the book: gospel or letter?

    B. Structure of the book

    C. Summarization of the plot

    D. The implication of your pericope's location in the book

IV.   Pericope Analysis Exegesis

    A. Genre or literary type of the passage

    B. Explain the importance of where your passage is located within book's structure

    C. Thought by thought

    D. Summarization of the passage

V.   Appropriation-Application

VI.   Expository Sermon

An Exegetical Study of Romans 6:1-7

In this section, *The New Revised Standard Version* is utilized.

Rom 6:1-7

[1]What then are we to say? Should we continue in sin in order that grace may abound? [2]By no means! How can we who died to sin go on living in it? [3]Do you not know that all of us who have been baptized into Christ Jesus were baptized into His death? [4]Therefore we have been buried with Him by baptism into death, so that, just as Christ was raised from the dead by the glory of the Father, so we too might walk in newness of life.

[5]For if we have been united with Him in a death like His, we will certainly be united with Him in a resurrection like His. [6]We know that our old self was crucified with Him so that the body of sin might be destroyed, and we might no longer be enslaved to sin. [7]For whoever has died is freed from sin.

2

<u>Chapter Two: Introduction</u>

WHY STUDY THIS PASSAGE?

ROMANS 6:1-7 PRESENTS the apex of the epistle. Herein, Paul shows the reality of our need for salvation in Jesus. He shows why we need salvation and how that takes place. Life without God will end in His eternal wrath. However, the one who applies faith to God's grace will not be the objects of His wrath. Rather, they will walk in a proper relationship with Him.

Jesus has freed us from the punishment of our sin by becoming our atonement. We have been justified – pardoned, acquitted – from our sin through His death, and thereby we have been set free from the power of sin.

In Rom 6, Paul shows how Jesus overcame the power of sin. Paul describes sin as having power over the children of Adam. However, the power of sin is broken for those in Christ – the *second* Adam. Therefore, those who are in Christ have been crucified with Christ and are no longer under the power of sin or enslaved to sin. They have been set free and are now enslaved to Christ. The theme of the chapter is freedom *from* the power of sin and freedom *in* the power of Christ. We are described as slaves *to* Christ who bought us from slavery to sin – then set us free.

THESIS STATEMENT

This passage, Rom 6:1-7, crowns the epistle. It explains what has happened to the believer in the spirit, teaches the believer who we are in Christ, and guides the believer on how to implement Christ's power in our life. This is a transition from what God has accomplished to how this will be lived out in our daily lives –

3

moment by moment.

Chapter Three: Historical Context

AUTHOR, AUDIENCE, DATE, OCCASION

ROMANS WAS WRITTEN to the Christians of Rome by the Apostle Paul (1:1) during his third missionary journey. Written about A.D. 55, Paul was in Corinth, living at a friend's house, at the time he wrote this letter.[1] Paul never actually went to Rome until his imprisonment.[2]

Paul usually did not address his letters to someone personally (cf. I Corinthians; II Corinthians; I and II Thessalonians; Philippians; Ephesians and Galatians). He would only greet persons by name in epistles written to congregations he had not yet visited. In Romans and Colossians, for instance, Paul does greet some individuals he personally knows by name. It appears that he would add personal greetings to some letters, not because they were private, but because he intended to show the readers that, as a friend of these persons, he was trustworthy.[3] This would be similar to a minister today showing his license, to demonstrate that this denomination approves of his ministry.

This letter seems to indicate that Paul sees a transition point in his ministry. For over twenty years, he had been planting churches

---

1 John F. Walvoord, Roy B. Zuck and Dallas Theological Seminary, *The Bible Knowledge Commentary: An Exposition of the Scriptures* (Wheaton, IL: Victor Books, 1983-c1985), 2:436.

2 Even at this time he almost did not make it. They were shipwrecked and Paul was able to minister to the solders, prisoners, and natives. For more information see Hans Betz Dieter, "Paul," *Anchor Bible Dictionary,* 6 vols., Edited by David Noel Freedman, (New York: Doubleday, 1992), 186-201.

3 Charles F. Pfeiffer, and Everett Falconer Harrison, *The Wycliffe Bible Commentary: New Testament* (Chicago: Moody Press, 1962), Rom Introduction.

in the eastern Mediterranean. Now he is writing to the church in Rome. There is, however, much controversy as to why Paul wrote to the Romans.

There are three main theories suggesting possible reasons:

1. Some believe the book is a list of Paul's missionary plans. He desires to visit Spain by way of Rome. With Spain at the end of the world for these people, Paul may have wanted a community of faith located somewhere central to his journey. Some scholars feel that the church at Rome would fulfill that function. This theory derives from Paul's "resume," given in Romans 15:22-24.

2. Others believe that this is a compendium, or summary, of

3. Paul's theology. I feel this may not be true because of the doctrinal directives omitted from the book, including: The Lord's Supper, the Second Coming, and an explanation of the purpose of the Church.

4. Yet others believe that the book is Paul's pastoral response, indicating that he was aware of the local problems within the church: libertinism, abuse of grace, abuse of strong drink, dietary disputes (such as the consumption of pork), and arrogance. It seems, therefore, that Paul writes this letter to remedy these concerns.[4] With this work, Paul seems to show his theological strengths as a "pastoral theologian."[5]

---

4 Class notes, "Intro to Rom," Lee University, Cleveland: TN., fall 2003.

5 C. Kavin Rowe, "Apostle of the Crucified Lord: a Theological Introduction to His Letters," (The Christian Century, Nov 30, 2004), available<http://www.findarticles.com/p/articles/mi_m1058/is_24_121/ai_n8702473> (29 November 2006).

Despite the theories, we do not really know the reason. Paul wrote this Epistle.

SOCIOLOGICAL, CULTURAL, AND RELIGIOUS BACKGROUND

Paul is a unique and very intelligent man. His amazing personality and aura of strength demonstrated the goodness in his life. His character was so strong that those who came into contact with him, either in person or by letter, were compelled toward Christ. The Christians in Rome were powerfully moved by Paul's teaching.

He was both well-respected and exceptionally hated. Writing the letter to the Christians in Rome, Paul did something very uncommon sociologically for this time. He wrote a letter addressed to a particular community, at a particular time. They probably were not expecting to get a detailed run-down of his doctrine. Paul may have done this because most of his Roman readers had never met him but were familiar with the reputation of his ministry (both good and bad).[6]

It is believed that Rome was founded on the Tiber River in 753 B.C. Rome was founded here because the hilltops could be used during battle. This must have worked well for them, because by Paul's day, Rome was the largest and most powerful city in the world. This vast empire of approximately one million people was the political hub of world trade. Paul did not begin this Christian community in Rome, but it is believed that many of his converts and friends moved to Rome (Romans 1:5–6, 13; 11:13; 15:15– 16).[7]

6 Stephen Esterholm, Understanding Paul: The Early Christian Worldview of The Letter to The Rom, 2nd Edition, (Grand Rapids: Baker Academic, 2004), 9-13.

7 Robert B. Hughes, J. Carl Laney and Robert B. Hughes, *Tyndale Concise Bible Commentary, Rev. Ed. of: New Bible Companion*, 1990.; Includes Index., The Tyndale reference library (Wheaton, Ill.: Tyndale House Publishers, 2001), 521.

With the population growing rapidly, having the chance to preach in Rome would have been a great ministry opportunity.

Chapter Four: Literary Context

GENRE OF THE BOOK: GOSPEL OR LETTER?

T HOUGH HIGHLIGHTING MANY elements of the Gospel, this book is most definitely an epistle addressed specifically to the believers in Rome. New Testament scholar Christopher Bryan asserts that the epistle serves several functions: a Greco-Roman letter; an essay about healing; a rhetorical sermon; an instruction on intimate relations; and a letter explaining condemnation.[8]

STRUCTURE OF THE BOOK

This epistle is an exhortation from the Apostle to other believers to engage in holy living. This letter pours from Paul's heart as a pastor. It is a personal, hand-written letter by Paul to the church at Rome.

Paul wrote the Epistle in *Koine* Greek, the language form common to the "working class" of the Roman Empire. Paul relies on rhetorical styles common to the time and introduces them to Scripture. Paul begins with a greeting followed by a blessing. Then comes the body followed by a salutation (doxology).

FLOW OF THOUGHT

Before we go any further, we need to gain an overall view of the book as a whole:

1. Opening statements of Paul, the chief Apostle (1:1-17).

2. Righteousness, proper relationship to God (1:18–8:39).

---

8 Christopher Bryan, *A Preface to Rom: Notes on The Epistle In Its Literary And Cultural Setting*, (Oxford, New York: University Press, 2000), 11-41.

3. God's plan for Israel and the Gentiles (9:1–11:36).

4. Expectations for the Christians at Rome (12:1–15:13).

Jesus came into this world as a man, bringing the gift of God's grace to us. Rather than death by sin, we receive life - eternal life – from Christ. Sin is to death what righteousness is to eternal life in Christ. We inherited death from the *first* Adam. We inherit life from the *second* Adam.

We are not merely *with* Christ (as friends or troops might, for instance, congregate), but we have been united *in* Him (much like two fluids combine when mixed). Though verses 1-4 of Romans 6 highlight this union, we will be focusing specifically on verses 1-7, where Paul describes the great mystery of our freedom from sin.

At the outset, Paul seems to contradict himself: "we who die are alive." This is the theme of this section.[9] It seems ridiculous – even impossible. Yet upon closer examination, he is not conflicted.

Paul is outlaying the amazing paradox that exists in our topsyturvy world – the paradox that we, living, were dead in sin; and now we, dead, are alive in Christ. We were dead *in* sin as sons of Adam.[10] Now as sons of God, we are dead *to* sin which had enslaved us, and are alive *in* Christ. We are now more bound to Jesus than we had ever been bound to sin. We are so bound to Christ that in His death we also die, in His resurrection we also rise, and in His life we also live.

We in Christ are created to live an eternally righteous life. Paul urges us to walk diligently in this truth – as slaves of Christ and not of sin.

---

9 This is a reoccurring theme throughout Paul's writings.

10 The masculine mode used here is meant to be viewed in the universal sense and is used as such to engender readability.

TIMOTHY R. CARTER

THE IMPLICATION OF THE PERICOPE'S LOCATION IN THE BOOK

In these verses, Paul shifts our thinking from what Jesus did in relation to *God* to what Jesus did in relation to *us*. He shows us that, while Jesus accomplished something for us in the past, He continues working for us in the present.[11]

---

11 Larry Richards and Lawrence O. Richards, *The Teacher's Commentary,* Includes Index, (Wheaton, Ill.: Victor Books, 1987), 815.

CLASSICAL EXPLANATION of SALVATION

Chapter Five: Pericope Analysis Exegesis

IN THE FIRST four chapters, Paul is writing about God and His righteousness. He explains that the foundation for salvation is justification by God's works – not by man's works. We can be justified only by faith in Jesus Christ. In chapter 5, we hear Paul explain how sin came into the world and held humans in bondage. Jesus then defeated sin on the Cross, and salvation gives us peace with God.

In chapter 6, we learn about what actually takes place in the Spirit and what gives us this peace. We also learn of sanctification. In chapter 6 we find the unifying factor of the letter, tying together the process of salvation with the fullness of the Spirit referenced in chapter 8.

Chapter 7 continues to lay out sanctification. Chapter 8 shows us how we can walk after the Spirit of God. In chapter 9, Paul explains that the election of grace is for all who accept Jesus. In chapters 10 and 11, we see that salvation is offered to everyone. Finally, chapters 12 through 15 instruct us on how to live as lights for Christ, both towards each other as believers and towards society as a whole.

Unification with Christ Stops the Misuse of God's Grace (v.1)

Paul begins this section by asking a question. Within this question he confronts the horrific doctrine put forward by some in the Roman church – that we may sin freely because grace is offered freely. In v.1, Paul uses the Greek word which is often translated as "remain" or "continue". In either case, this word denotes an ongoing action.

He uses the Greek word, often translated as "sin", which can be translated either as "sin" or "being evil." In using this word, Paul is not speaking of any specific sin, but rather all sin in general.[12]

Let us here take a closer look at sin. If we do not first understand *sin,* we will not understand this passage. Notice that sin is not merely a collection of actions or unrighteous deeds. Sin is a fundamental rejection of God and God's grace. Sin is the rejection of the image of God created in humanity. It is an affinity for the destruction of that image where it appears in mankind. Notice that God Himself was not tarnished or diminished in any way, but the imagery of God *in Adam* is now distorted in some manner. Sin is a rejection of God's love and a failure to return to love. Sin is living in opposition to the revealed will of God.

Paul also makes use of the Greek word which can be translated as "kindness," "good will," or "favor toward someone." This Greek word also describes "grace." Grace is sometimes misinterpreted by evangelicals as being merely a cover for sin – as if we sweep it under the rug and God can no longer see it. True grace, however, is far more. Grace does not simply forgive. It is the power of God given to us to live a life *without* sin.

Let's Do God a Favor by Living a Sin-filled Life (v.2)

In verse 2, Paul shows his utter disgust with the corrupt doctrine that is being considered. Paul uses the words which are translated as "come to exist" or "become." One important note is that Paul places a prefix in front of this Greek word. This negates the meaning of the word. The Greek prefix is usually translated as "not," or "By no means!" In the Greek, we can see that this prefix strikes a note of shock, anger and surprise. For example: "WHAT?!!!?"

---

12 W., Günther, *The New International Dictionary of The New Testament Theology,* 6 vols., ed. Colin Brown, (Grand Rapids: Zondervan, 1971). 573-83.

This is a result of the issues previously raised (3:8). Paul seems to scream, "By no means," in reference to Christians who have died with Christ and who live in Christ. The life of a believer should show the life of Christ, in victory over sin and death. Paul shows the contrast between two Greek words (translated as "died", and as "life"). This shows the contrast between life and death in the life of the believer. Here again we see the Greek word for "sin" – as above.

We are Judged Dead to Sin, yet in Christ we Live (v.3)

In verse 3 Paul teaches about baptism using the word inflection, which is translated as, "wash, assumedly by dipping, in a ceremonial way," and "baptize, to ceremonially cleanse, with the visible agent of water, to show purity and initiation into Christ through repentance."[13] We have been baptized, showing that this has already happened. As an explanation of what it means to be a part of Him, "into" is to be translated as "into Christ." This shows that we are actually a part of Christ. The believers were baptized to show that this happened to the believer – not by anything we have done but by what Christ has done. In addition, it explains the unity we have with Christ now. Another word to note is the Greek word which is translated as "death" or "plague." This is to demonstrate the contrast between our life and our death. Moreover, this is to show the contrast of our life and death to the life and death of Christ. This word in the Greek is in the past tense, tying in with verse 2 as the symbol of baptism. This is analogous to how in verse3 "to die to sin" demonstrates that we are judged dead to sin in Christ.

---

13 James Swanson, *Dictionary of Biblical Languages with Semantic Domains: Greek (New Testament)*, electronic ed. (Oak Harbor: Logos Research Systems, Inc., 1997), GGK966.

This is the Beginning of the Turning from the Curse of Sin (v.4)

There are three main views of this baptism in verse 4:

1) The first suggests that the baptism is not an actual physical baptism in the water, as we practice as part of our sacraments. Rather, this metaphor represents what takes place in the life of the Christian. It also gives an understanding of what takes place in the Spirit. This is not water baptism, but spiritual baptism. The Christians in Rome would not have considered water baptism as an option here.

2) The second theory is that this is a metaphor which helps the believer understands what has taken place in the spirit. This shows a complete break from the old life.

3) The third view indicates that the believer is buried with Christ and shows the involvement the believer has in this baptism with Christ. This focuses on the uses of the word which is translated throughout Paul's epistles as "bury together with." This shows that the believer is placed alongside Christ in baptism. "With Him" shows how He fulfilled this in us. Thus, just as the Spirit of God is present during the sacrament of the Lord's Supper, then the Spirit is also present during the sacrament of baptism in the same manner.[14]

This word is translated as "baptize," indicating a permanent change. This was used in the secular setting, meaning to dip; to plunge; a violent aggressive act; a ship sinking; a person who drowned; or the pickling of a vegetable.[15] We can also view "baptize" as the cup of God's wrath that was placed on Jesus (Mark 10: 38, Luke 12:50).

---

14 Douglas Moo, The New International Commentary on The New Testament: The Epistle to the Rom, (Grand Rapids: William B. Publishing Co, 1996). 361-64.

15 James Montgomery Boice, "Baptism," *Bible Study Magazine*, May 1989.

Imperatively – Jesus crucifies our flesh and we are called to follow Him. Eschatologically – we have the blessed hope of physical and spiritual resurrection in the future, "Arise oh sleeper!" Notice also the words that are translated as "into the death," to show that this happened to us, not by anything we have done; but by what Christ has done. Moreover, this phrase explains the unity we have with Christ now. This is not physical death but a spiritual death and, in addition, shows again the contrast of death and life. Paul lays out a powerful phrase that is translated as "also we in newness of life might walk around," or, "so we too might walk in newness of life." This is to show that He overcomes the power of death by the power of God; likewise, we too will overcome the power of death only by the power of God.

United with Him in Death and Resurrection (v.5)

In verse 5, we see the phrase translated as "Have been united," which shows that this happened to the believer not by anything he had done, but by what Christ has done. This wise Apostle chooses a powerful word showing that we are grafted into Him so that we together with Him will live as One. Since we are grafted together, what happens to Christ must also happen to us. The best way to understand the term "united" is to consider fruit breeding.

Fruit Breeding

Fruit breeding, often called "hybridizing," is the horticultural process of interbreeding two different (but genetically compatible) types of plants so that they produce a new type with superior characteristics. This process can often be seen with pitted and citrus fruit. Many common fruits, such as nectarines, were produced through hybridizing, but while interbreeding can produce superior fruits, generating results is a time-consuming and unpredictable process. Hybrid seedlings may take ten or more years to flower and to bear fruit on their own roots.

Grafting, on the other hand, can reduce the time needed to bear fruit, shortening the interbreeding program.[16] Mature branches from one fruit type can be grafted to the root stock of another, allowing cross pollination during flowing. New varieties, then, can be bred within months rather than years.

The Grafting Process

Grafting is an artificial technique of vegetative reproduction, in which a small branch or bud of any desired plant is inserted into the root stock of another plant. This is called, "plant propagation."

If a budding twig from a pear tree, for example, is carefully inserted into a slit made in the bark of a quince bush, a pear branch will grow. The quince bush, then, will bear both pears and quinces. Though strange results may emerge, grafting has become a vital agricultural technique.

After the graft heals, the new plant becomes *a single living entity*. Though sometimes used to save the life of a mature plant, grafting is most often used to accentuate specific plant characteristics in order to produce some desired result. For example, a variety of peach tree may tolerate sandy soil better than some varieties of plum; thus, plum branches grafted to peach root stock would enable the propagation of plum orchards in sandy soil conditions.

Grafting has been used for thousands of years, mostly for olive trees, and was well-known to the people of biblical times. Some varieties of olive trees had very vigorous roots but produced poor quality olives and vice-versa. To create hardy plants with desirable fruit, branches that produced good-quality olives were grafted onto trees with stronger root stock, creating an altogether superior olive

---

16 "Plant Breeding," available at <*en.wikipedia.org*/wiki/Plant_breeding> (March 4, 2011).

tree.

Though several grafting methods are used to insert the budded twigs or scions (living shoots) into the stock of another plant, two rules must always be followed:

1. Firstly, only related species of tree or shrubs can be grafted. This implies that apples can be grafted onto pear and quince trees; peaches can be grafted onto an apricot, almond, plum or other stone fruit trees; but apples cannot be grafted to peach trees.

2. Secondly, the cambium layer which carries the vital sap of scion must touch the cambium layer of the stock on which it is grafted. If it does not, the grafted twig cannot grow.

The technique of grafting is also widely applied in the case of animals and human beings. Used within plastic surgery, grafting procedures routinely save lives. For instance, surgeons can take bone material from a rib and graft it into the nasal bone to reconstruct a damaged nose or pull healthy skin from one part of the body to replace the damaged tissues of burn patients.

One Tree Producing Fruit of a Different Tree[17]

Grafting is a beautiful illustration of our unification with Christ. Through grafting, one tree begins to produce the fruit of a different tree, and in Christ, we begin to "bear fruit" that resembles that of our Savior.

---

17 Brigid Gaffikin, "Grafting Fruit Trees Can Be Simple," *San Francisco Chronicle*, available <www.seattlepi.com/nwgardens/435594_Fruittrees16.html> (March 4, 2011).

We are now one with Christ, just as He is one with the Father.

This is an answer to Jesus' prayer, "…Holy Father, protect them in Your name that You have given Me, so that they may be one, as We are one" (John 17:11). Because we are united with Christ, we are expected to live a godly lifestyle. Paul makes this clear, not only in this epistle, but in others as well (for a case in point, see Titus 2:11-15).

Paul explains that all people are expected to live godly lives, shunning ungodliness. In Titus, Paul uses the Hellenistic rhetoric to create a polemic against the common strands of the culture. Paul used the language, but redefined it to the Christian faith.[18] This is the same thing he did in Romans. He reconfigures the regular writing styles of the culture, making them Christian.

Though united with Christ, we do not become gods. We do not become the Trinity. We become holy as He is holy. We become intimate with the Trinity. The Trinity is One. The doctrine of the Trinity teaches about the intimate relationship within the triune Godhead. Father, Son and Holy Spirit take pleasure in a divine love and respect for one another for a divinely united purpose. The Bible shows examples of these personal relationships within the

Trinity during the baptism of Jesus (Matt 3:13-17; Mark 1:9-1; Luke 3:21-22; John 1:29-34).[19]

---

18 William D. Mounce, Word Biblical Commentary: Pastoral Epistles, Vol 46., (Nashville: Thomas Nelson Publishers, 2000). 421-22.

19 For a short explanation on the unity of the Trinity see, Kenneth Archer and Melissa Archer, "The Doctrine of The Trinity," *Church of God Evangel*, Vol. 96, (Cleveland, TN: November 2006), 6-8.

Crucified with Him (v.6)

In v.6, Paul continues to use powerful language with the word translated as "was crucified together." This word is a verb, aorist, passive, indicative, third person, and singular. This shows that this is an action that has taken place in the past. It is important to notice that Paul explains, *"the old of us man was crucified together,"* or better yet, as the NRSV puts it, "our old self was crucified." This did not happen to us as believers, but it happened to our old sinful "self." This is not a deed that the believer *does;* rather, it was *done to* the believer. This structure also shows that crucifixion happened to Christ on the cross, but the effects still remain today! The crucifixion is not *ongoing,* but Christ applies the effects of the crucifixion to our old selves. If we have a struggle with something, we do not need to question our salvation. Rather, we need to pray for His grace. This reveals that the believer is converted, not merely in *part,* but in *entirety.*

Crucifixion in first century Rome was humiliating. The rich and popular were never crucified. Rome almost never punished a Roman citizen by crucifixion. Crucifixion was usually reserved for foreigners, slaves, disgraced soldiers, and Christians. This process would take anywhere from six hours to four days to bring the victim to death. The victim usually died from cardiac arrest, brought on by all the pain, torment, and humiliation they experienced. The Roman guards were not allowed to leave the site of the crucifixion until the victim had died. Sometimes the guards would speed up the process by breaking the victim's bones or by driving a spear into his heart. Guards might also have hastened death by building a fire at the foot of the cross – suffocating the victim. [20]

20 "Cilliers L, Retief," (PubMed-indexed for Medline), available: <http://www.ncbi.nlm.nih.gov/entrez/query.fcgi?cmd=Retrieve&db=PubMed&list_uids=14750495&dopt=Citation> 2003 Dec; 93(12):938-41, (28 November 2006).

Roman Crucifixion was a public display of mockery. In Colossians (2:14), we see that Jesus crucified our sin by nailing it to the cross. Jesus Himself was nailed to the cross. When Jesus nailed our sin to the cross, we know that He was making a public mockery of Satan. This is what is taking place in our flesh. Our old self (this is our flesh, our nature that goes against God) was crucified. At the cross in Christ's crucifixion He made the provision for us to become crucified. When we accept Him as our personal Lord and Savior, we are accepting the provisions and joining with Him in the provisions that He has made. This crucifixion happened by Christ on this cross, but the effects still remain today!

The word which is translated as "abolish, cause not to function," or "might be destroyed" is a verb, aorist, passive, subjunctive, third person, and singular.[21] This shows that it is not a definite *fact,* but a definite *probability.* However, it demonstrates that the definite probability has in fact taken place. This means that this action had happened to the old sinful nature. The action is past; having happened at a particular moment in time. The action happened only once at this point of time. It will never happen again. The point of time where this old sinful nature was destroyed occurred on the cross. Jesus nailed our sin to the cross.

With Christ and Freed from Sin (v.7)

Practically repeating verse 6, in verse 7 Paul emphasizes what it means to be crucified with Christ and freed from sin. The one who free from sin is the same one who had died with Christ. Paul is illuminating that the one who participates with Christ in His death, burial, and resurrection is thereby justified. Paul repeats his point to infuse it into the reader. Paul has summarized vv. 1-6, setting us

---

21 William D. Mounce, *The Analytical Lexicon: To the Greek New Testament,* Zondervan Greek Reference Series, (Zondervan Publishing House, Grand Rapids, 1993).

up for the logical "next step" he will introduce. Christ severs the hold sin has over the believer through death. According to a familiar Jewish proverb, when a person is dead, they are no longer expected to keep the Law.[22] Thus, free from the law in death, we are free to live in Christ.

We humans are created in the nature of God, but we all sin. Yet, the believer is a new person in Christ Jesus. Justified by His obedience to the Father, and humbling Himself to become a man, Christ created the possibility for sinners to be recreated - through redemption. When we accept Christ, we become new creatures with new lives (John 5:24; Romans 6:11; Ephesians 2:1–6). Though redeemed once, we are continually renewed by Christ (2

Corinthians 4:16; Romans 12:1 and 2); and now that we are in Christ, we have eternal life through Him (2 Timothy 4:18; 1 Peter 1:4; John 14:2 and 3).[23]

SUMMARIZATION OF THE PASSAGE

In Romans 6:1-7, though Paul has not yet been to Rome, he has the heart of a pastor and so confronts the warped theology that had begun to infect the minds of the believers in Rome. By this, Paul shows the reality of our need for salvation in Christ. We learn of the need for salvation and what actually happens in the spirit when we are saved.

Life without God will end with the eternal wrath of God. Jesus has freed us from God's wrath by becoming our atonement. We have been justified – pardoned (acquitted) – from our sin. We have been set free from the power of sin. Paul explains our union with Christ;

22 W. Burrows, The Preacher's Complete Homiletically Commentary: on the Epistle of St. Paul The Apostle to The Rom, (Grand Rapids: Baker Book House, 1980), 168.

23 Guy P. Duffield and Nathaniel M. Van Cleave, *Foundations of Pentecostal Theology* (Los Angeles, Calif.: L.I.F.E. Bible College, 1983), 14244.

we are crucified, buried, and resurrected with Him by the power of God. Therefore, we are no longer bound in slavery to the power of sin but have been enslaved to His power — and set free.

APPROPRIATION-APPLICATION

Romans 6:1-7 should be applied to our life by our accepting what Christ has done for us. We show the power of life in Him by living a life freed from sin, dedicated to Jesus and holy living. We as believers are not compelled to commit vile actions that offend the known will of God. We as believers are not forced to obey

God's will either. We have the ability to choose whether we want to accept and follow Christ; whether to obey God's will or to oppose His will.

Once we have accepted Christ as our Lord, we are united with Him. Our lives, united with Him, will show a Christ-like quality. The more we refuse to sin, choosing instead to obey God, the more we become like Christ. Christ crucifies our desires to disobey God. As He crucifies our desires, we show this crucifixion by exhibiting the fruit of the Spirit in our lives.

Some very precious truths emerge from this chapter. One truth is that we must die to live. Having been united with Him, we also partake in His suffering. Because He fulfilled the Law in death, in Him we died because He was just and lives; in Him we live.

In Galatians chapter 2, Paul says that he himself was crucified with Christ, yet lives; and Christ lives *through* him. Because of the life of Christ *in him*, Paul continually chooses to live freed from sin. Because Jesus died, we can live.

The best way to make the correct choice is to remember that we have been bought by His blood and united with Him. Our "old man" is dead and we have been united with Christ in His life. As described above, grafting dramatically illustrates what occurs when we are implanted into Christ. We, foreign "plants," are permanently placed into a new, living root system (Christ). He becomes our sole source of life and power. We are not merely attached. We become a new part of the original —and the root (Christ) provides all we need to successfully live our new existence.

Think about the process of planting seeds. We place the seed in the ground and cover it up. The seed will have then been buried, just as Christ was buried in the tomb. We give these seeds the proper amount of water they need to grow. What is actually happening in the grave? What is happing to the seed? This seed will begin to decay; the outer shell will break away, separating from the embryo. As the embryo sprouts roots, a root system is developing to stabilize and feed the new plant.

As its struggle begins, this will develop into a stem. The stem will war against the covering of the grave persevering to the surface. Upon its resurrection, it springs forth into a new plant. A new life due to the baptism, a death has taken place causing the seed to die. Just as we die with Christ to bring forth new life.

What is it that Paul is really saying here? Paul is letting the believer know that it is not by our works but by the finished work of Jesus that we are saved and remain saved. We as believers are called to know what Christ had already done and by faith let our lives show His finished work.

We are not awaiting a blessing from Him; rather, we have already received the blessing of eternal life. We are not to live in fear of tomorrow, but to rejoice for today and tomorrow as we look back at what Jesus has done. Crucified, He set us free. We are children of God and no longer slaves of Satan – compelled to do his bidding. We need to recognize that we have been set free from our old dead selves and are alive in Christ. We are rich with His grace!

Chapter Six: The Sermon: Understanding Salvation

Letter about the Sermon

WRITTEN TO BE preached to the typical congregation, the following exegetical sermon from Romans 6:1-7 is intended to challenge us to search our hearts. If we harbor any sin, we should repent. As we examine our lives, we will discover whether we are slaves to sin or united to Christ. This sermon lays out the mystery that takes place in the spirit when we are saved. The understanding of how Christ pleased God and redeemed us will empower us to live in the truth that we are not doomed to toil in sin but are free to live justly.

Outline for The Sermon: Understanding Salvation

Romans 6:1-7

  I.   Introduction

  II. Unification with Christ stops the misuse of God's grace

  III. Let's do God a Favor and persist in sin so that God's grace will be abundant, and He will be noticed more!

  IV. This is the beginning of our turning from the curse of sin.

  V.   Crucified with Him

  VI. Severing of body and old nature

  VII. Closing

The Transcript

INTRODUCTION

Locate with me Romans 6:1-7

I will be reading from the *New King James Version.*

The purpose of this sermon today is to explain the biblical teaching of death and separation from the old sinful nature. The title of this message is "Understanding Salvation." The passage that we will be studying tonight is a difficult passage. I am going to explain in a simple manner some of the technical things I have found in the Greek. Please bear with me. I believe by this we will be able to gain a better understanding of God's Word.

Before we read this text, for a few minutes I want to talk about sin.

What is sin?

What does the word "sin" mean?

Sin comes from an archery (bow and arrow) term. When the archer pulls back the bow and releases the arrow, he has a target in mind. If he misses the target, then he has "sinned." Using the word in this manner does not mean separation from God; it does not mean anything Christian. It simply means the archer missed his mark.

We use this word because God has a target for us. We as believers are aiming to God's goal for us. God's goal for all of us is that we be conformed to the image of His son, Jesus Christ (Romans 8:29). If we do not follow this Gospel that He has provided, then we cannot come into the image of Christ; therefore, we will miss the mark. If we miss this target, then we are sinning.

Sin is living in opposition to the known revealed will of God.

He shows His will to us in many ways. He reveals His will by the work of the Holy Spirit in our lives. The Holy Spirit will convict us and guide us into the path that God desires for our life. He has exposed His will to us in His Word. This Word is inspired by God. Every dot, every mark, every period, every exclamation point, every word – every bit of this word is inspired by God! This Word is the known will of God. It is the revealed will of God, shown to us by inspiration of the Holy Spirit. We need to obey this Word, or we are sinning.

Why does sin bring such an offence? Why is it that God wants us to obey His word? Didn't Jesus die once on the cross for all sins? So that means, then, that because He already died once for all sins, we can continue sinning, right?

No, this is not correct! We will deal with that issue in a few minutes.

Let's talk about how sin first came into the world. Sin entered this world by Adam. We see in Genesis that he is created as a perfect, pure person. He is created in the image of God. Adam did not know sin. He did not know corruption or anything wrong. He did not know anything outside of his relationship with God. Sin entered the world by the human's volitional ability, which allowed Adam and Eve to sin. A human's volitional ability is the ability the human has to choose. We do not have to obey God. We do not have to love God. We have the ability to choose something different from the will of God as He reveal it to us. The first sin, the sin of Adam, is a result of his being able to choose to obey God or to not obey God.

Adam only had one command from God, "Do not eat from the tree of the knowledge of good and evil." Eve gave Adam a piece of fruit from this forbidden tree. He, knowing full well that God told

29

them not to eat from this tree, chose to disregard God's command and eat of the tree. Adam disobeyed the known and revealed will of God this brought sin into the world.

Adam had a close, undefiled relationship with God. He had such a pure relationship with God that, when he broke this relationship, he disrupted all humanity. All people after Adam are born into sin. It is not just that Adam disobeyed, but that Adam disobeyed and broke mankind's relationship with God. Adam had been created in the image of God, but when he disobeyed – when he broke this relationship – he also tarnished the image of God in which he was created. He became as one who had sinned and could no longer shine with the pure, undefiled image of God.

Now all creation has been affected by one man's sin. All humanity, after Adam, is born under sin. The very nature of the human is sinful. The foundation of humanity is now rooted in Adam's sin.

Sin is relational. As believers, we have a relationship with God only through Christ. Because of sin, the original relationship between humans and God is broken; it is no longer complete as God desires. The relationship with God was not as we need it to be until the coming of the second Adam, Christ Jesus.

Notice! Sin is not a collection of actions.

Sin is a rejection of God and God's grace.

Sin is a rejection of the image of God and the destruction of humanness. Notice, God Himself was not tarnished or diminished in any way. Nevertheless, the *imagery* of God that is in Adam is now distorted in some manner.

Sin is a rejection of love; a failure to love.

Sin begets evil!

Sin is a rejection of God's way.

Sin is not merely a list of the traditional seven deadly sins:

Pride is the excessive belief in one's own abilities, interfering with the individual's recognition of the grace of God. It has been called "the sin from which all others arise." Pride is also known as vanity.

Envy is the desire to possess others' traits, status, abilities, or situation.

Gluttony is an unreasonable desire to consume more than that which one requires.

Lust is an inordinate craving for the pleasures of the body.

Anger is manifested in the individual who rejects love and opts instead for fury. It is also known as wrath.

Greed is the desire for material wealth or gain, ignoring the realm of the spiritual. It is also called covetousness.

Sloth is the avoidance of physical or spiritual work.

Yes, these are sins; each one of these things is a sin. But sin cannot be fully described by a simple rendering of these seven vices. Sin is not limited to a cut-and-dried list.

Sin can be understood as a broken relationship with God.

This broken relationship with God is sin.

Sin has consequences but God has provision! The Bible tells us,

Romans 6:23

[23]For the wages [consequences] of sin is death; but the gift of God is eternal life through Jesus Christ our Lord.

Sin is alienation from God. When we sin, our position before God as a righteous person is changed. When we sin, we are stepping away from the position of righteousness. We are away from God. God's answer for this is reconciliation (Romans 5:10).

Sin is bondage to evil. God's answer for this is redemption (Romans 8:2).

Sin is condemnation for the guilty. God's answer for this is justification (Romans 5:18).

This is what I was just talking about. The alienation brings condemnation, but the justification brings us back to the correct position with God. Justification replaces us into the position of righteousness in God's sight.

Depraved humans cannot save themselves; we do not have the ability within ourselves to fix the problem. We cannot sing enough songs. We cannot preach enough sermons. We cannot come to the altar long enough, hand out enough tracts, or tell enough people. We cannot draw enough pictures or write enough books to fix the problem. Because we are depraved, we lack the ability to save ourselves. We are hopelessly bad. Our salvation is, "not by works lest any man should boast" (Ephesians 2:9). God's answer for this is regeneration (Romans 6:4-6).

Sin is eternal death for the sinner. God's answer for this is eternal life (Romans 6:23).

Sin exercised dominance in death. God's answer for this is grace, which also exercises dominion through justification, leading to eternal life through Jesus Christ our Lord (Romans 5:21).

Paul points out that, as sin increases in humanity, God provides more grace for humanity.

Paul then says in Romans 6:1-7:

¹What shall we say then? Shall we continue in sin, that grace may abound? ²God forbid. How shall we, that are dead to sin, live any longer therein? ³Know ye not, that so many of us as were baptized into Jesus Christ were baptized into His death? ⁴Therefore we are buried with Him by baptism into death: that like as Christ was raised up from the dead by the glory of the Father, even so we also should walk in newness of life. ⁵For if we have been planted together in the likeness of His death, we shall be also in the likeness of His resurrection: ⁶Knowing this, that our old man is crucified with Him, that the body of sin might be destroyed, that henceforth we should not serve sin. ⁷For he that is dead is freed from sin.

Paul is writing this epistle to the believers. He writes in Chapter 5 about how sin entered the world through humans – how the very foundation of our makeup has been corrupted because of

Adam's disobedience. Paul explains that Adam and Eve were in perfect union with God. Adam was human and without sin, but he did not obey God. He did not follow God's desires but looked to his own desires. He decided to make his own decisions, not fully believing God's decree promising death. This is sin entering the world because of Adam's decision to follow after his own desires. Thus, all who come after Adam are born into sin.

Romans 3:23

²³For all have sinned, and come short of the glory of God; Does this mean that all of us have sinned?

Yes! All of us have sinned and have fallen short of God's glory (Romans 3:23).

What does this mean: *Sin entered the world?* What is sin? Sin is living in hostility to the known will of God.

Does this mean that, because we are humans, we are sinful?

That our biological makeup is sinful? That is to say that it is a sin to be human. Paul says, "NO!" It is not a sin to be human, but it *is* the nature of man to go his own way and to not take into account God's ways. To fail to obey the will of God – this is sin! It is allowing our desires to work against God's will that makes us sinners. It is our disobedience to God's Word that makes us sinners.

So, Paul poses some questions.

UNIFICATION WITH CHRIST STOPS THE MISUSE OF GOD'S GRACE (Romans 6:1).

¹What shall we say then? Shall we continue in sin, that grace may abound?

(v.1) "Should we continue in sin in order that grace may abound?" As I mentioned earlier, it would misuse God's grace to intentionally continue in our sin, so that God's grace increases. Think about it. Would it bring God more glory if we sin more because His glory supersedes our sin? For me to commit all seven deadly sins would certainly show God's grace, because the more I sin the more His grace abounds – right? NO – NO! Let's see what the text says about this.

LET'S DO GOD A FAVOR AND PERSIST IN SIN SO THAT GOD'S GRACE WILL BE ABUNDANT AND HE WILL BE NOTICED MORE!

²"God forbid. How shall we, that are dead to sin, live any longer therein?"

(v.2) No! This thought should never enter your mind! Paul says, "By no means! How can we who died to sin go on living in it?" We shouldn't entertain these ideas. Paul seems to be screaming that he is offended and shocked that a believer would think such an evil thought. How can we continue in our own desires, when we have died to ourselves, giving up our own desires? Having accepted the work that Jesus has done for us on the cross, how then can we live in the sin for which He was nailed to the cross? We cannot live in sin and also be a believer. It cannot be done, and this is what we will be dealing with for the rest of this sermon. Our liberty – our faith – is not a license to sin! But our faith gives us cooperation with God as He gives us His grace, which empowers us to live a life without sin.

[3]"Know ye not, that so many of us as were baptized into Jesus Christ were baptized into His death?"

(v.3) Here is a truth that is very often overlooked: we are judged dead to sin, yet in Christ we live.

This word "baptized" should be focused on. The word

"baptized" was a secular term that meant "a violent act taken upon a person or something that changes the direction of, changes the appearance of and/or that changes the purpose or direction of something." For example, if a ship were to hit a rock or an iceberg its direction would be violently altered. Notice this is not caused *by* the ship but is something that happened *to* the ship. When the ship goes under the water, we say the ship sank – or "was baptized." There was a violent occurrence, which changed the direction of that ship.

John the Baptist obviously took the secular term, "baptism," and used it to describe what was happening in the spirit. The nature of a man was to make his own decisions, to exercise his own will – but there was a violent act being done to the human. The human did not do it, but it was done to him. This sudden, forceful act changed the character, or direction, of his nature. He was baptized unto Christ and unto His death. This means that now we are dead to the person we once were. The believer has become united with Christ.

In the text, we hear Paul saying that we "have been baptized

into Christ Jesus." This is not saying that we are inside of Christ – like we are inside of this building. Rather, this is saying we are inside of Him so much so that we have *become a part* of Him. Being inseparable from Him, being united with Him, being grafted together with Him, we are being fused together with Him into His very being. This is the heart of being baptized unto Christ. This we are not doing to ourselves, but Him doing to us. He made the provision for this on the cross, and the effects continue to this day in our lives. This is God's work in us.

THIS IS THE BEGINNING OF OUR TURNING FROM THE CURSE OF SIN.

[4]"Therefore we are buried with Him by baptism into death: that like as Christ was raised up from the dead by the glory of the Father, even so we also should walk in newness of life."

Water baptism is a symbolic act of worship, showing a testimony of what has happened to the believer in the spirit. As a believer is submerged under the water, he symbolizes his death to the world and to the sinful life in which he once lived. As the believer is held under, he signifies his submission to Christ. And as he is raised from the water, he demonstrates his resurrection as a new creation in Christ.

Though we are in Him, Christ is not being resurrected again with each baptism. When He was baptized by John, it was not a sign of His regeneration, but an expression of His redemptive power. His baptism foretold of His ability to redeem us and pictured our unity with Him in spirit. Water baptism is not only a testimony of what has happened to the believer in the spirit, but it is a celebration of the installation of the new believer into the Christian community of faith.

As the believer takes the first breath after coming out of the water, he signifies the rebirth of his spirit. As the believer opens the eyes for the first time after coming out of the water, he pictures the spirit man who was blind and now can see. "I once was lost but now I am found." As the believer, having been bathed, comes out of the water, he exemplifies the spirit man who, once dirty with sin, is now washed in the blood of the Lamb!

[5]"For if we have been planted together in the likeness of His death, we shall be also in the likeness of His resurrection:" In verse 5, we find an important word, the word "united."

What does "united with Him" mean? Does it mean that I have my name on the church roll? Does this mean that I have the reputation in the community of being a "good Christian?" Does this mean that I go to the store and pass out tracts? Is this being united with

Christ? No, this is not. Being "united with" Christ is of equal importance with the word "baptism," and implies becoming one with Christ. It gives the idea of being dead and buried, as Christ was also buried in the tomb. Now, the believer is baptized unto Christ and partakes in His death. This "united" means "to come together, to come into being, to begin to grow as one."

Let us shed some light on this subject. This "united" could be understood through the process of fruit breeding. If you were to take two different varieties of citrus fruit – grapefruit and tangerine, for instance – and cross-breed them, you would create a fruit called a "tangelo." This popular hybrid fruit is a product of hybridization, the process by which the pollen of one plant is used to fertilize the flowers of a different plant.

The problem with hybrids, however, is that when you plant the seeds of a hybrid, they may or may not produce the hybrid plant. Some will revert back to the parents' characteristics. In the case of the tangelo, planting tangelo seeds will produce some tangelos, some grapefruits, and some tangerines. The only way to consistently propagate tangelo trees is through a process called

"grafting." Tangelo sprigs are inserted into the trunk of a compatible tree variety, and the branches eventually grow to produce tangelo fruit.

This is how the grafting process works.

The gardener would select a number of compatible, healthy citrus trees and cut them to stumps that terminate just a couple feet from the ground. He would then collect a number of live shoots from a tangelo tree and trim them so that each length has several buds. He would carve one end of each stem (or scions, as they are called in gardening circles) into a tapered wedge.

Once all of the components are prepared, the gardener will wheel through the orchard with his scions. He will cleave each stump approximately in the middle, then place two scions into the split, taking care to make sure that the cambium of each scion contacts the cambium of the root stock.

The cambium, by the way, is the "living" area of the tree. This is the "growth ring" that lies just under the bark. The cambium supplies nutrients to the entire tree, and if cut or damaged, can lead to the death of the entire tree.

Once the scions are implanted, the gardener secures the graft, then seals it with wax. Over time, the grafts that "take" become a living, unified part of the tree. They become inseparable, and damage to the grafted branch can harm the entire tree.

They are no longer *two* plants, but *one*.

Another Example

Think about the process of planting seeds. You place the seed in the ground and cover it up. The seed is now buried, just as Christ was buried in the tomb. The seed is dead, lifeless, hard. And then what happens? As we supply the right moisture and light, this seed will begin to soften; it will absorb water and expand. The outer shell will break away, separating from the embryo. The embryo sprouts roots, implanting itself in the ground. With roots providing stability and nutrition, the new plant is empowered to battle its way to the surface.

Resurrected in new life, the seed, once small and powerless, becomes a vital force, strong enough to pierce granite. Without the "death" of the seed, as Jesus said, an awe-inspiring new plant could not grow. The seed, dead and buried, springs forth in *new life*, just as our death with Christ brings forth new life in us. Paul says that is what took place in the life of a believer when he was buried in the grave with Christ.

When we are baptized into Christ, we become one with Him, just as a graft becomes one with the root. We produce one fruit - the fruit of the Spirit of Christ, which is love, joy, peace, patience, kindness, generosity, faithfulness, gentleness, and self-control (Galatians 5:22-23).

How then can we continue in sin? How can we pridefully demand our own way when we have become united with Christ within our very nature? We have been forever cut off from our old selves and have been joined eternally with the nature of Christ.

"For if we have been planted together in the likeness of His death, we shall be also in the likeness of His resurrection" (v.5). We are representations of Christ in all we do. Because He is risen, we are to walk triumphantly in the reality of our resurrected life in Him!

"CRUCIFIED WITH HIM"

The phrase, "crucified with Him," indicates that, at a *specific* point in the past, the believer was crucified. We did not crucify our "old" selves (v.6). We were crucified with Him by *His* act.

⁶"Knowing this, that our old man is crucified with Him, that the body of sin might be destroyed, that henceforth we should not serve sin."

This word "crucified" differs from the word "baptized." While baptism signifies a sudden act of violence, crucifixion signifies the suffering that leads to death. Remember when Jesus was on the cross between the two thieves? Death did not come instantly. Death arrived in slow, agonizing spasms. Crucifixion illustrates our powerlessness in the face of sin's destruction (6:6).

The crucifixion was the display of public humiliation and mockery. In Colossians 2:14, we see that Jesus crucified our sin by nailing it to the cross but Jesus Himself was nailed to the cross. We see also, in the next verse, that when Jesus was nailed to the cross, He made a public mockery of Satan. This is what is taking place to our flesh. Our old self (this is our flesh, our nature that goes against God) was crucified, and we gained victory over Satan.

When we accept Christ as our personal Lord and Savior, we are accepting His victory over sin and joining with Him as justified before the Father. Therefore, if we struggle with a "besetting sin," we do not need to question our salvation, but rather we need to seek His grace. (His grace is strength to live a life without sin.) If, however, we *love* our sin, we *should* question our salvation.

In my paraphrase, Ephesians 2:1-10 tells us that we were once dead through the trespasses and sins in which we lived, being a slave of the enemy of God. We were, by our very nature, children of wrath but God loved us "even when we were dead through our trespasses."

By grace, through faith, we have been saved and brought to a new life in Christ.

Notice that verse 6 does *not* say "*was* crucified." Paul writes "*is* crucified." By this, Paul reveals, "We know that our old self was crucified with [Jesus]." This evidence of the continual virtue of the crucifixion (that we are continuing to die to sin) gives us hope – the confidence that our futures promise holiness.

Within the phrase, "*is* crucified *with* Him," we see that our old self does not *perform* the action. Rather, our old self *receives* the action. It is important to understand this reality. We do not crucify ourselves. We have been placed by the Spirit into Christ, and we have then been crucified with Him by the Father. Salvation is not something *we* must do – it is something God has done *for* us!

The crucifixion of our flesh is a slow, agonizing process! We continually face public mockery. The Spirit infuses us with the wisdom to make Godly decisions. Our sin nature has been rendered powerless! Our flesh no longer has authority over us because we have submitted ourselves unto the baptism of Christ and have been united with Him. Christ has become our authority! Hallelujah! The power of sin has been struck down. The believer is progressively changed – day by day – as the Holy Spirit sanctifies us.

SEVERING OF BODY AND OLD NATURE

Now the sin nature and the flesh is already defeated, but still tries to gain power over us. This is again different from being baptized. The sin nature struggles to regain power. If it were not struggling for power, then there would be no reason for Romans 8, where Paul admonishes us to "not walk after the ways of the flesh" (verse 4). He encourages us to not submit to our flesh, but to submit to the ways of the Spirit just as we face a war in our spirits,

Paul speaks of a "war in [his] members." Paul's desires fight to satisfy themselves. In the Spirit, however, he fights his desires.

James tells us that when a man sins, he is being led away by his own desires:

James 1:14

¹⁴"But every man is tempted, when he is drawn away of his own lust, and enticed."

In Paul's spirit, there is a severing taking place between his old nature that loves sin, and the new nature that loves God. He recognizes this. It's almost like the "old man" never got the death certificate.

This is taking place within us today, is it not?

Can we not see in our own lives how we battle sin and how we desire to put away our old selves in submission to God?

We must stay before the Lord in prayer; submit to Him; ask

Him for His guidance. Though dead in the spirit, our flesh isn't going away without a fight. The practical death of our flesh is a long, throbbing, drawn out, brutal, humiliating and excruciatingly painful process.

Our flesh is dying slowly, just as Christ died slowly on the cross for our salvation. For this reason, Paul continues in verse 6, "... crucified with Him, that the body of sin might be destroyed, that henceforth we should not serve sin." The way this is worded in the Greek suggests that the phrase, "might be destroyed," is not a definite *fact* but a definite *probability*. This verb is used in a way that shows the significance of time in the process. It shows an undefined action that took place at specific point in time. We do not really know *when* this is *actually* happening. We believe that the point of time which made it possible for this old sinful nature to be destroyed occurred at the cross.

This word, "destroyed," is a very strong word. It shows strong emotion. Paul rejoices in the fact that sin is being destroyed. Sin is being absolutely annulled! The body of sin has been overpowered and utterly decimated. It cannot control us anymore! We were once slaves to sin – but *NO MORE*! The body of sin is continuously being destroyed by Jesus by way of crucifixion!

Sin enslaves – but Holy Spirit empowers!

Sin enslaves the person to do the bidding of sin's desires.

Holy Spirit empowers us to do God's desires!

[7]*"For he that is dead is freed from sin."*

There is a result to this crucifixion. Suffering will stop. When the suffering stops, we will no longer war against sin because it will be completely destroyed in every way. We will be completely submitted to the authority of Christ, "For he that is dead is freed from sin" (7).

We are no longer united together with sin. The believer has died to sin. In this context, the ones dying are those who are crucified with Him. Therefore, the death mentioned here would be death with Christ. For whoever had died with Him is already freed from sin.

Sin no longer has the authority as we submit our lives to Christ. We are putting to death the deeds and desires of our own authority and coming under the authority of Christ. If we have not done this, we are workers of lawlessness. "Lawlessness" is being a law unto ourselves.

Matthew 7:22-23

[22] Many will say to me in that day, Lord, Lord, have we not prophesied in thy name? and in thy name have cast out devils? and

in thy name done many wonderful works? [23] And then will I profess unto them, I never knew you: depart from me, ye that work iniquity.

Jesus is explaining how some will come to Him claiming to have performed many deeds for His glory on which they rely as their "credentials" for entering His presence.

Jesus in essence responds, "Get away from me! I have never been intimate with you because you are a law unto yourself."

The Greek phrase that is translated as "ye that work iniquity" is often translated as "lawlessness," which means to not obey the moral or civil law. It also means to disobey God while being enslaved to the Antichrist ("the lawless one" – 2 Thessalonians 2:8).

We also see in the book of Matthew that sin *is* lawlessness.

We understand that many things are sin. Lying is a sin.

Dishonoring our parents is a sin. Taking the name of God in vain is a sin. Sin itself is spurning God's law and substituting our own. The understanding here is that, when we make the decision to make ourselves the authority in place of God – just as Adam did in the garden – we become separated from God. For this reason, Paul exhorts us to stand with Christ in the new life we have been given instead of standing with the old, dead man.

CLOSING

As we close, I encourage you to remember — our flesh was killed – destroyed – by Christ in the crucifixion. In His resurrection, we were given new life – a life freed from slavery to sin. So, let us not live as slaves, but as freed men and women, living in the truth of our power to life righteously. We are free to walk after the Spirit. Cooperate with Christ as He crucifies our flesh daily. Even though it can be a long, painful process, remember – "This, too, shall pass!" The suffering will come to an end.

Let us have a word of prayer!

PRAYER:

"Heavenly, Father, thank you for this opportunity to study your Word. Thank You, for being the God who has suffered for us and invited us to come into Your family; uniting us together with You and with one another. We ask You, to help us to follow after You, walking after Your Spirit, putting away our desires and accepting Your authority in our lives. In Jesus name, Christ, You are King! Amen!

CLASSICAL EXPLANATION of SALVATION

Chapter Seven: Saved by Grace

WHEN WE ARE saved, what are we saved from? We are saved from sin and the punishment for sin. If we are not a new person, then we are not saved. But when we are saved, all things are new.

When we are saved, we are not a sinner anymore because we have been washed clean by the blood of Jesus Christ.

I am not aware of any place in the Bible where the Church, the people of God, are called "sinners." The closest is Paul's wellknown reference to himself as the "foremost" (or "chief") of sinners in 1 Timothy 1:15.

Paul is saying that he knows that he needs Christ more than any other person.

Paul tells us that he is the worst of all sinners just after he explains that at one time, he was a blasphemer, persecutor, and violent enemy of Christians (1 Timothy 1:13).

Because he now understands salvation in Christ, he knows how much he is dependent upon Him.

Let's look at a few verses about our identity. In John 3:6 Jesus states that those who are saved are born of the Spirit. In 2 Corinthians 5:17 we are a "new creature" or a "new creation".

Galatians 2:20 tell us Christ lives in us and Colossians 1:27 says God has now made known the mystery of Christ in us. 1 Peter 1:23 is clear that we were born again...

CLASSICAL EXPLANATION of SALVATION

Chapter Eight: Compare Saved to Sinner

SAVED OR SINNER? Think about our words. Our Christian identity is in Christ; *not* in sin!

We find in the New Testament that the people of God have been given many titles. They are the "elect" (1 Peter 1:1), "faithful brothers" (Colossians 1:2), "beloved" (1 John 2:7), "children of God" (1 John 3:2), a "holy nation" (1 Peter 2:9), and most of all they are called "saved."

This does not mean that Christians do not sin. Christians do sin. This means that the sins of a Christian are much deeper and more serious than we often realize. This is the whole point of Romans 7, where Paul explains the fact that he often does what he does not want to do. The entire Christian life is a struggle between the new self and the old self. Unfortunately, our old self often wins out. Paul can even refer to himself as a "wretched man" (Romans 7:24).

Paul even tells us that whenever he sins, it is not Paul that is doing it. He explains, "So now it is no longer I who do it, but sin that dwells within me" (Romans 7:17). And again, "Now if I do what I do not want, it is no longer I who do it, but sin that dwells within me" (Romans 7:20).

Paul is not trying to make up some excuse where he is not guilty of these sins by reason of having a split personality. No, Paul knows he is responsible for these sins. This is his struggle. Sin is not committed by the new nature, but by the *old* nature. Paul is admitting that because he is now saved and understands the accomplishments of Christ's work, he is even more culpable than he was in his ignorance of Christ.

Our identity is now bound up in the new man that has become a slave to Christ. The old man is being crucified, just as Christ was crucified.

Effect of Sin

What effect does sin really have?

The devastating proof of the effect of sin is what God did in order to stop sin. Sin could not be stopped by the sacrifice of animals. It could not be stopped by the will power of humans. It took the power of Christ suffering, blood and death to stop sin.

We should calculate the severity of our sins, realizing that each person is in danger of eternal punishment because of sin. We conduct this calculation by understanding the cost of our salvation. We cannot truly perceive the price Jesus paid in order to secure our eternal life with Him. Jesus would not have left Heaven, suffered, and died if the power of sin was not great. His actions, His suffering, His agonizing crucifixion, His death is the only way to strip sin of its power.

Nobody can be both a saved person, child of God and also be a sinner. Because every person who commits sin without repentance—because the reward for sin is death.

But the reward in Christ is "eternal life".

Romans 6:23: For the wages of sin is death, but the free gift of God is eternal life in Christ Jesus our Lord.

Nobody can be both a Saved person, child of God and also be a sinner. Because every person who commits sin without repentance does not have a good relationship with God.

Isaiah 59:2: Rather, your iniquities have been barriers between you and your God, and your sins have hidden his face from you so that he does not hear.

Nobody can be both a saved person, a child of God - and also be a sinner, because every sinner is a child of the devil.

1 John 3:8: Everyone who commits sin is a child of the devil; for the devil has been sinning from the beginning. The Son of God was revealed for this purpose, to destroy the works of the devil.

Every person who commits sin without repentance is guilty of rejecting the authority of Christ and setting themselves up as their own authority, "lawlessness".

1 John 3:4: Everyone who commits sin is guilty of lawlessness; sin is lawlessness.

Nobody can be both a saved person, child of God and also be a sinner. Because every person who commits sin without repentance is on the way to death not eternal life.

James 1:15 then, when that desire has conceived, it gives birth to sin, and that sin, when it is fully grown, gives birth to death.

Paul Calls Believers Saved

Paul refers to believers as saved. Christians have the choice to follow Christ in righteousness, or to commit sin. A sinner does not have the choice to do works of righteousness. We should think of ourselves in line with our new natures, not our old natures. We are those who are saved who sometimes choose to sin; not sinners who sometimes do right.

We need to understand our true identities in Christ. This actually affects the way we view (and respond to) the opportunity to commit sin. If we think of ourselves as "sinners", it can actually have a negative effect on us. We could start to believe that our sins are an ordinary part of life. Maybe you have heard someone say, "Well everyone sins a little bit every day." No, that is what "sinners" do. Sinners sin - that is what makes them sinners.

We should view ourselves as "saved," then we will begin to see our sin in a whole new light. Sin does *not* have control over us any longer. Sin is no longer our master. Christ is now our master.

Sin, then, is even more wrong and even more vile because it is being done when we now have new natures and a new identity in Christ. This is why Paul can honestly classify himself as a believer in Christ, (one who has received the forgiveness of Christ) and at the same time 'the chief of sinners' (1 Timothy 1:15). Paul knows the difference between being a slave to the sin and having accepted the forgiveness of Christ; for this reason, his sins are that much more disturbing.

We can finally be set free from the burden of sin, but if we do not comprehend what that means (and if we have no one to teach us) then we will be placing ourselves inescapably in the position of resorting to our old ways.

When we are saved from sin, Christ breaks the power, the authority of sin and we do not have to obey sin anymore. Yet we still have a choice to commit sin or to choose righteousness.

We Christians should see ourselves as saved from sin. We should also be glad to think of ourselves as saved. After all, this is the reason Christ came to earth.

When Christ returns, He is coming for those who are saved. In glory, there will be no sinners. Only saved. He is coming for those without a blemish.

These are those who did not defile themselves with sin but remained committed to Christ. Ephesians 5:26-28 (NRSV)

"…in order to make her holy by cleansing her with the washing of water by the word, [27] so as to present the church to himself in splendor, without a spot or wrinkle or anything of the kind—yes, so that she may be holy and without blemish. [28] In the same way, husbands should love their wives as they do their own bodies. He who loves his wife loves himself."

Chapter Nine: If You Don't Know Christ

IN THIS SECTION *The Message* and the *New Living Translation* are utilized.

GOD HAS A MESSAGE FOR YOU...

...and it's a great message, the kind that puts a smile on your face. His message is simple – yet life-changing. A genuine response to His message will trigger an immediate impact.

It is not often you receive a message that helps pave the way to your eternal destiny.

If you think God's message to you is filled with anger and wrath, you are in for a pleasant surprise. God is *not* out to "get you"! In fact, His heart's desire is to bless your life with good things. Jesus said, "I came so you can have real and eternal life, more and better life than you ever dreamed of" (John 10:10).

Think about that for a moment, God wants your life to be an outstanding adventure! He wants you to enjoy the good life. Now *that* is a message I can live with. But it doesn't stop there; He has so much more to say. God's message is...

A MESSAGE OF LOVE

"This is how much God loved the world: He gave His Son, His one and only Son. And this is why: so that no one need be destroyed; by believing in Him, anyone can have a whole and lasting life" (John 3:16).

You are loved unconditionally! You might say, "I've heard that all my life, but I don't feel loved! I have never experienced it. My life is one flop after another, one lapse after another, one failure after another. If God really loves me, if His love is available to me, where is it? How do I experience it?"

Think about this - God has it all. He owns it all. As Psalm 50 says, all the animals of the forest, the cattle on a thousand hills, every bird of the mountains... "All creation and its bounty are mine [the Lord's]" (Psalm 50:12). He could give you anything — money, possessions, prestige, success, a life of privilege. He could give you anything — but what He wants to give you *most of all* is the ability to know His love.

Love is God's greatest resource. He takes love so seriously that He defines Himself by it. The Bible says "God is love" (1 John 4:8). God loves you far more than any parent could love a child. As saved Augustine said, "God loves each of us as if there were only one of us."

If you want to experience the love of God, all you have to do is ask Him. He will shower you with irrevocable, unconditional love.

A MESSAGE OF PURPOSE

The search for purpose in life has puzzled people for thousands of years—thus, we usually look in the wrong places. Rather than look to God, we look to ourselves. While society and self-help books disagree, you won't discover purpose by looking within yourself. Only God, the creator of life, can reveal your purpose here on earth. "Everything, absolutely everything, above and below, visible and invisible…everything got started in Him and finds its purpose in Him" (Colossians 1:16).

To know God's purpose for your life requires that you know God. God desires to have a relationship with you and show you your purpose in life, but sin has separated man from God. In order to restore man's relationship with God, He sent His Son Jesus Christ to die for you and pay the penalty for your sin. Because the penalty for sin has been paid, you can have a relationship directly with God, but it requires an individual response from you to receive it.

A MESSAGE OF ACCEPTANCE

Society can be cruel, and for some people rejection is an ongoing reality. You long for genuine connection and a warm embrace but cannot find it. Your search for significance can lead you into a lifestyle you really do not want to live. It happens to us! We go to bed at night, put our heads on our pillows, and say to ourselves, "How did I get like this? I cannot believe I turned out like this!" In that moment, when we are at our lowest point, we feel like no one will ever really accept us. Are you ready for some great news? God will accept you, just the way you are! At this very moment, He is thinking about you. In fact, His thoughts toward you are as numerous as the grains of sand (see Psalm 139:18). If you could count every grain of sand, the number would not match how often He thinks about you. You are the apple of His eye and His arms are open wide to receive you into His warm embrace.

The love of God, His purpose and His acceptance are available to you right now, but to accept Jesus into your heart you have to acknowledge that you are sinful: "For everyone has sinned; we all fall short of God's glorious standard" (Romans 3:23 NLT). Once you have made that acknowledgement, the rest is easy...

- Be willing to repent and turn away from sin "For the wages of sin is death"(Romans 6:23 NLT).

- Believe that Jesus Christ died for you on the cross "But God put His love on the line for us by offering His Son in sacrificial death while we were of no use whatever to Him" (Romans 5:8).

- You must receive Him "But to all who believed Him and accepted Him, He gave the right to become children of God" (John 1:12 NLT).

Receiving Christ into your heart is as simple as asking Him to come into your life. You could pray a simple prayer like this:

Pray with me:

"Dear God, I know that I am a sinner and need your forgiveness. I believe that Jesus Christ died for my sins. I want to turn from my sins. I invite Jesus Christ to come into my heart and life as my personal Savior and Lord of my life. In Jesus' name,

Amen."

Now that you have received Christ into your heart, you have become a child of God. You can talk to Him in prayer at any time about anything. The Christian life is a personal relationship with God through Jesus Christ. Please find a good Bible believing church to attend on a regular basis.

Bibliography

Aland, B., Aland, K., Karavidopoulos, J., et al, Editors. *The Greek New Testament with Greek-English Dictionary (Ancient Greek Edition)*. Stuttgart, Germany: Hendrickson Pub, 2006.

Archer, Kenneth and Melissa. "The Doctrine of The Trinity," *Church of God Evangel*. Vol. 96, Cleveland, TN: November 2006.
Brown, Colin. *The New International Dictionary of the New Testament* Grand Rapids: Zondervan, 1971.

Boice, James Montgomery. "Baptism." Bible Study Magazine. May 1989.

Bryan, Christopher. A Preface to Romans: Notes On The Epistle In Its Literary And Cultural Setting. Oxford, New York: University Press, 2000.

Burrows, W.. The Preacher's Complete Homiletical Commentary: on the Epistle of St. Paul The Apostle to The Romans. Grand Rapids: Baker Book House, 1980.

Class notes. "Intro to Romans." Lee University, Cleveland: TN., fall 2003.

Dieter, Hans Betz. "Paul," *Anchor Bible Dictionary*, 6 vols. Edited by David Noel Freedman, New York: Doubleday, 1992.

Duffield, Guy P. and Nathaniel M. Van Cleave. *Foundations of Pentecostal Theology*. Los Angeles, Calif.: L.I.F.E. Bible College, 1983.

Esterholm, Stephen. Understanding Paul: The Early Christian Worldview of The Letter to The Rom, 2nd Edition. Grand Rapids: Baker Academic, 2004.

Gaffikin, Brigid. "Grafting Fruit Trees Can Be Simple." San Francisco Chronicle.<www.seattlepi.com/nwgardens/435594_Fr uittrees16.html> available, March 4, 2011.

Hughes, Robert B., J. Carl Laney and Robert B. Hughes. *Tyndale Concise Bible Commentary,* Rev. Ed. of: New Bible Companion, 1990.; Includes Index., The Tyndale reference library. Wheaton, Ill.: Tyndale House Publishers, 2001.

Moo, Douglas. *The New International Commentary on The New Testament: The Epistle to the Rom.* Grand Rapids: William B. Publishing Co, 1996.

Mounce, William D.. *Word Biblical Commentary: Pastoral Epistles.* Vol 46., Nashville: Thomas Nelson Publishers, 2000.

_____. *The Analytical Lexicon: To the Greek New Testament.*

Zondervan Greek Reference Series. Zondervan Publishing House. Grand Rapids, 1993.

"Plant Breeding," <en.wikipedia.org/wiki/Plant_breeding> available, March 4, 2011.

Pfeiffer, Charles F. and Everett Falconer Harrison. *The Wycliffe Bible Commentary: New Testament.* Chicago: Moody Press, 1962.

Rowe, C. Kavin. "Apostle of the Crucified Lord: a Theological Introduction to Paul and His Letters." (*The Christian Century*, Nov 30, 2004. <http://www.findarticles.com/p/articles/mi_m1058/ is_24_121/ ai_n8702473> available, 29 November 2006.

Retief, Cilliers L.." (PubMed-indexed for Medline). <http://www.ncbi.nlm.nih.gov/entrez/query.fcgi?cmd=Retrie ve&db=PubMed&list_uids=14750495&dopt=Citation> 2003 Dec; 93(12):938-41, available, 28 November 2006.

Richards, Larry and Lawrence O. Richards. *The Teacher's Commentary*. Includes Index. Wheaton, Ill.: Victor Books, 1987.

Swanson, James. *Dictionary of Biblical Languages With Semantic Domains: Greek* (New Testament. Oak Harbor: Inc., 1997.

W., Günther, T*he New International Dictionary of The New Testament Theology,* 6 vols., ed.

Walvoord, John, F.. Roy B. Zuck and Dallas Theological Seminary. *The Bible Knowledge Commentary: An Exposition of the Scriptures*. Wheaton, IL: Victor Books, 1983-c1985.

Willmington, H. L.. *Willmington's Bible Handbook*. Wheaton, Ill.: Tyndale House Publishers, 1997.

About the Author

T IMOTHY CARTER WAS born in North Georgia, USA, to loving parents. He is the second of three children raised in this pastoral home. He has served as Pastor, Assistant Pastor, Counselor, Prison Chaplin, Ministerial Care Director, President of the Ministerial Association, Professional Speaker, and Storyteller.

He is the author of several books, blogs, newspapers, and international journal articles.

Carter holds degrees of Bachelor of Science in Pastoral Ministries, with a concentration in Counseling from Lee University (2005); Master of Divinities with a concentration in Counseling from Pentecostal Theological Seminary (2008).

Carter is a Bishop with Church of God, Cleveland, TN.; License Community Service Chaplain; Licensed Level 4 Church Consultant; Christian Counselor.

Books by Timothy R. Carter

Classical Explanation of Salvation

Credit Repair: Your Comprehensive Guide

Ditch the Junk: How to Have a Successful Yard Sale

How to Grow Through PTDS: A Guide for Personal Growth Through Stress

Vision: See it Achieve It

LARGE PRINT Word Search: The Gospel of Matthew

Connect with the Timothy R. Carter

Web site: TimothyRCarter.com

Facebook: https://www.facebook.com/Timothy-Carter-Author-499971137072277/?ref=settings

Blog: https://www.facebook.com/timothycarterbooks/

Twitter: @TimothCarterPhD

Amazon: amazon.com/author/timothycarterphd

<u>Notes</u>

Made in the USA
Columbia, SC
29 November 2021

49840905R00039